TABLE OF CONTENTS

PREFACE

As an adolescent, I helped my siblings with their homework assignments. My mother oftentimes thanked me for helping them when they whined and complained to her about not knowing how to do something, and she wasn't able to help them herself. I knew then that this was a calling that echoed in my brain until my twentieth birthday. In 1998, I joined the ranks of Substitute Teachers in Nashville, Tennessee. A ten-year career began, and that experience has led me to write this book.

I can remember one of many days in my beginning years. What became a pet peeve of mine in this facet of teaching was the fact that teachers sometimes failed to leave accurate lesson plans or leave any at all. A coordinator of special services at the Board of Education once mentioned taking along a "bag of tricks" just in case no plans were left. We all understand that emergencies occur and last minute unexpectancies don't always allow for preparedness. Much like the southern floods that hit Nashville and surrounding counties recently in our state, we must be prepared for those unexpectancies. However, when those failures arise, Substitutes find themselves in a great and irritating bind. Bam! The door slams open. In come the students, and you have nothing to assign them once the bell rings. Should you pull out tricks from that bag? If so, what tricks would be fitting to your young audience? Grades you may be teaching may range from prekindergarten to the twelfth grade. Do you have tricks that would suit each one of these audiences?

This book is designed to prepare the first-time professional for the unexpectancies that stop you dead in your tracks and that may hinder progress. That hindrance has caused some to completely stop dead in their tracks and cease working in the field. It is hoped these suggestions herein will equip you to run that race of teaching for teachers and students with endurance so that you'll reach that finish line and achieve your short-term or long-term goals to become one of the best Substitute Teachers around that teachers and administrators alike will request to have in their schools and classrooms on a regular basis.

Furthermore, these suggestions are designed to help the Substitute who mainly prefers working in the elementary school setting. However, many suggestions may also be used in the secondary school setting as well.

GETTING STARTED

Your first steps in becoming a Substitute Teacher are to gather your college credentials, state identification cards, such as a driver's license and social security card; and then head to your local Board of Education. Logging online to Google or Ask.com should point you in the right direction if you don't know the whereabouts to the location of that Board. A phone call beforehand may prove valuable to you to ensure you have all items necessary to meet the requirements. Complete the application and get the name of the person who accepted it for your personal records. If a copy of it can be made free of charge, ask for it. If charges apply, pay the twenty-five to fifty cents. Believe me, it will be well worth it to have it on-hand should it get misplaced. A week should be sufficient to wait for the application to be reviewed by staff and Human Resources. If no one has contacted you, a follow-up phone call will show them how much you desire the position. Most departments have an insufficiency of available Substitutes and would jump at the opportunity to hire people who actually want to do this difficult job.

Once your foot is in the door, and your first assignment has been accepted, it's time to go compose teacher report sheets. I have used my own, but a quick search online could lead you to other options. You want to start by using an Excel worksheet page listing the following:

Student Name
Absent?
Behaviors?
Sick?
Early Dismissal?
Office Visit?

At the bottom of this form can be footed:

D = Disrespect to Teacher
F = Fighting
I = Incomplete Classwork or Homework
L = Lunchroom Behavior
O = Other_____
S = Specialty Class Behavior
T = Talking at Inappropriate Times

The back of the page can be halved into two parts detailing lessons covered and/or work assigned. The other side can be the personal letter to the teacher thanking him for choosing you to work for him and letting him know about any emergencies needed to be mentioned or an explanation about any extreme activities at the school or extreme behaviors from one or many of the students. It is recommended that this report sheet be double-sided and not to have too many pages for the teacher to read. Being blunt and straight to the point will suffice. If he needs more explaining, the two of you can discuss things via telephone or even email if permissible.

Tip #1: Walking around the room and helping the students with their work is much better than remaining seated and sedentary. This not only helps you to get exercise but shows the students your interest in their educational well-being.

SUMMER HOMEWORK ASSIGNMENTS

A good idea is to take some refresher courses at your local junior or community college. If it's been a while since you've been in college, relearning the basics can assist you with those Math problems or remind you of the rules of proper grammar. This time when school is out can be used to compose additional classroom worksheets for all ages. Think about the ages you'll be working with and decide on assignments they should be able to do by certain grades. Also, if you choose to work with students with learning disabilities, it may also be wise to have on-hand simple assignments or activities they can enjoy.

ARRIVING AT THE SCHOOL

It was sometimes a headache for me after I got my assignments because they were not always offered before the day of the actual assignment. Sometimes phone tag was done, and this meant getting up early each morning, getting bathed and dressed for the day, eating breakfast, making supplications to God and prayer, and meditating on what the day lie ahead. When the assignments get called in at the last minute, though, these are the times when you'll have to be especially prepared to head straight out the door with that bag of tricks handy.

Once you get to the school, go straight to the administrative office. If your school district doesn't issue identification badges, you may get stopped in the halls by student personnel or even teachers. This shouldn't alarm you, but it could be irritating. To avoid any hassles, it's best to get a temporary badge from the office. Before signing any documents, wait for the school's secretary or correct office personnel to direct you to the correct sign-in sheet. This sheet serves as your timesheet for the day, so be sure to sign it appropriately with your legible handwriting indicating your identification number, first and last name, the teacher you have been assigned to work for, and the day's date. Inquire about the directions to the classroom so that you won't be walking around aimlessly trying to find it. If someone in the office is available to escort you, ask for this assistance. Moreover, make sure to obtain a key to the door so that you won't have to wait for the custodian to come and unlock the door. I found in my experience is they have so many things to do at the start of the day, it may take a while for them to get to you. It would be wise to already be in the classroom and settled before the students arrive so that you can compose yourself and familiarize yourself with your surroundings and classroom setting. Being in the classroom before the students arrive also gives you much needed time to look over the lesson plans and/or ask the neighboring teachers for assistance if there are no plans left.

Tip #2: Write your name on the chalkboard and a brief message about your expectations for the students in your care.

BEFORE STUDENTS' ARRIVAL

Once you get the room unlocked and gain entry into it, look around the room for posters and behavior modification boards and anything that gives you an indication of what is expected from the students. As soon as they arrive and see there is a Substitute present in their classroom, behaviors may manifest themselves right on the spot. Having a sense of authority that lacks fear should nip those in the bud instantly. If you take the time to look over the consequences of poor behavior, this can serve as reminders to them that you intend to deal with the behaviors and will enforce the consequences by any means necessary. The teachers next door won't want to be pestered or bothered by you when these types of situations get out of hand. This reminds me of what one of my teachers once told us students, "If you don't have anything to do, find something to do, or I'll find you something to do." We never want to look or seem like we can't do our jobs without someone looking over our shoulders. Administration has to complete clerical duties. The administrator and principal have to call parents, set up conferences, attend Board meetings, and discipline abrupt students. No other school employee wants to be distracted from his duties to help an incompetent Substitute Teacher. If this become habitual, the Substitute may get smiles and a "good job" from the staff but may secretly get a bad report sent to the Board of Education and not be asked to return to the school after they have left the building. Therefore, it falls heavily on the Substitute Teacher's shoulders to manage the classroom well. This also goes for those students who bully others. I recall a time when I had multiple jobs assigned to me from a teacher at an inner-city school. One student brought a gun to school for protection. This school, mind you, was an elementary school. However, the principal announced to all teachers, including Substitute Teachers, that we should all be on guard of any students who may be bullying other students so these could be disciplined and innocent students feel a sense of security.

See if the room is highly organized or if it's cluttered with books or even disheveled. Many teachers have distinctive organizational abilities. These become evident when you walk into their classrooms.

When the teachers have cluttered classrooms, though, it may rub off on their students; and, if you're like me, it can be quite annoying when you need to find items to use for the day but can't because of the untidiness of your surroundings. The time before the students arrive should be used to locate the lesson plans, scan over them as quickly as you can, organize and locate all needed materials for the day, and write a quick message along with your name and date on the chalkboard or whiteboard. When they arrive, they'll at least want to be able to see and read your name on the board if you're too busy to tell them at first start of the day.

FIRST THREE HOURS

What has worked for me at the beginning of the day is to immediately see what my morning time frame is. It could be that the students have a class to go to or even a special program the whole school has to attend in the school's gym or auditorium. Having this foreknowledge is valuable because it shows all the adults around you that you stay on your toes and on track of what's going on in the school. It could be that a "lockdown" occurs or even a "fire drill." Knowing what to do immediately without expecting anyone to tell you shows you to be the true professional and shows how protected children are in your care. In addition to wanting to be called back to the school by the one teacher you're working for at this time, you may even want another observative teacher to notice how hard a worker you are so that they too can call on you when they need you. Once they step foot in the door, though, you may want to say something like this, "Good morning! Please put your backpacks away, sharpen your pencil, and begin the worksheet on your desk." Once the first bell has rung, and most of the students have arrived, there may be just a few minutes before announcements begin. They can then be interrupted from their assignment, and you can introduce yourself to them. As long as there is nowhere else for them to go immediately, I go over the rules of the day, consequences, and all expectations. This has proven to put a healthy fear in them so that they know not to cross me. This may also prove helpful to you. Some children may still try you and test to see if what you said was true. To show other children you meant business at the start of the day when you went over the rules, you may want to put your foot down immediately and enforce what was previously stated. This will show the others that the same can happen to them if they try you too.

When you arrive early enough to be in the room before the students arrive, there is time for you to notice whether or not their specialty class is held at the beginning, middle, or end of the day. These specialty classes include Music, Physical Education or Gym, Art, Foreign Language, or any other such class where the students are away from you and in some other teacher's care for up to one hour.

This period of the day is otherwise known as the teacher's "planning" period. When you have this hour to yourself, it is not a time for you to read the newspaper or complete a crossword puzzle. This is the time for you to complete your report to the teacher, clean the classroom, organize their completed assignments, fill in their take-home folders, have a conference with the principal or other teachers about any concerns, and even sharpen the students' pencils. It is also an opportunity to read over the lesson plans that pertain to the remainder of the day. However, if this "planning" period is not until the end of the day, that time before the students arrive must be used to scan over all of the day's activities so that you can do everything timely and ensure they arrive to lunch and to their specialty classes on time.

Teach each lesson as best as you can. I recall being told in the orientation I went through at my hiring time that we weren't expected to teach like the classroom teacher. In my locality, only sixty semester credit hours were required to become a Substitute Teacher. Some states and counties require a bachelor's degree. However, a teacher's license is not required. Therefore, a Substitute is not required to teach exactly like one. Cover as much as possible within an allotted time frame. Be sure to give attention to all subject matter and don't spend too much time on one subject. If students don't get finished with everything, give them some time later during downtime to complete the assignments. Reward those who do complete early with a fun but educational activity.

When teaching Math lessons to elementary students just learning the basics, it may be wise to teach them to use their fingers. For example, 2+2=4. Put up two fingers with your right hand and two fingers with your left hand. Count both sets of fingers. Show them that they can do this when completing Math work and even when taking tests. Another finger helper is using fingers when multiplying. For example, most children learn how to count by twos, fives, and tens even before learning their multiplication facts. These can be repeated before going over the facts, and they can use their fingers. For example, 2x2=4. By putting up two fingers and counting each finger by two, they come to their product. This can be repeated with 5x2. This time, though, they would put up five fingers and count each by two. The product would, of course, be ten. Do you see how to do this? Lastly, for tens, 10x2=20. The smallest number of fingers would be put up. This would be the "two." Afterward, the student should be instructed to count those two fingers by ten. The product would be 20.

A spelling bee is a fun way to prepare the students for their spelling tests. This can be done any time before the test, even days before. For example, if you are working with the class on a Monday, and this test is scheduled for the following Friday, it wouldn't matter if you won't be teaching them that Friday; any extra help you give the teacher and the students in preparation to ace a test is always greatly appreciated. They could simply remain at their seats, stand in attention. When it's their turn to spell a word, they must spell it correctly. If they misspell it, they must sit down. The last student standing wins the spelling bee!

FIRE DRILLS

You're in the middle of teaching when, "rrrrng," the fire alarm goes off! What do you do? Where do you take the students? Unfortunately, this is not the time to be searching for that disaster plan that should have been easily accessible to you as you entered the room. If it's not posted on the door after you enter or even behind it, it's your sole responsibility to locate it. If it's not accessible, you must either inquire about the teacher's evacuation assignment with a neighboring teacher or contact the office to inquire about its whereabouts. Knowing exactly where to go will ensure that the administrators can find that particular bunch of children in your care. Also, having that list of students you wrote out on the report sheet at the end of this book will surely come in need. Always know how many children are in your care. Moreover, if a neighboring teacher became ill during the day or had some emergency to arise, their students may have been disbursed to other teachers around them. While it may not seem fair for you to get any additional students added to your care, you might get some anyway. These ones should also be added to your list as well as the number for a quick headcount. Take the students outside to the designated spot according to the teacher's directions. They are to line up in a single format. It may be the school's policy to have them turn and face the school. Silence is strictly enforced. When the administrator signals for the students to return to the building, make sure they all come back in with you and no one gets trampled on. Once back in the classroom, a good idea is for you to do another roll call to determine everyone has reentered the building and is where they should be. A note to the teacher at the end of the day is wise to leave in addition to other notations.

LOCKDOWNS

We live in a dangerous world. Though a school should be one of the safest places for anyone-especially children- sometimes what is called a "lockdown" is done when danger threatens the safety of them. There could be dangerous people inside the school. For example, a student who has exhibited poor behavior may get suspended or even expelled. Irate parents may demand that they not be so and cause disruption. Children, the administration can handle. Irate adults they can not. There may become a time when the proper authorities such as the police may have to be summoned and called to calm the matter. Crime could have been committed outside the school and in the surrounding area. A thief could have robbed a bank and escaped while the police is in pursuit of him. He could be running or driving near a school. When this happens, the rest of the building is "locked down," and the doors to the classrooms are locked as well as the entire building. No one trying to enter the building may enter, and students must remain in the classrooms. In addition to the students in your care, any students walking aimlessly in the hall must be pulled into your classroom. A roster should be available. If one is not, a manual one must be made. Usually, the administrator expects the Substitute to know what the procedure is at this time as it is similar at most other schools, and an announcement on what to do may not be made before the lockdown. Simply write out the names of the students in your care. The report sheet at the end of this book that you used at the beginning of your day can be used to access those names. Any additional students you pulled into your room need their names added to this list as well. A school personnel may knock on the classroom door and ask for this list if needed. An announcement will be made when the lockdown is complete. Continue teaching the students, though, and keeping them occupied with activities. There is no need to panic. They must remain inside, and, no matter how much they whine and cry, they must not be allowed outside of the room.

CLASSROOM VISITORS

All children in your care must be protected by you. Therefore, any visitors coming into the room should identify themselves. Though they should have signed in at the office and obtained a "visitor's badge," they should also sign in when entering the classroom. If the teacher you're working for doesn't have one, a sample one has been included at the end of this book. You could leave this for the teacher so that he will know who's been in his classroom while he's been absent. I recall working for one Music teacher who got robbed. His students turned in money for a field trip. I subbed for him in addition to several other Substitutes. When he returned, he called me to inquire about the money because he saw I cleaned the room. This would have been one of those times when a sign-in sheet would have come in handy. Any visitors who entered that room who didn't work for the Board of Education would have been identified and they may have been called instead of me! So, ensuring that the students are kept safe as well as the teacher's belongings will call for you to utilize a visitor's sign-in sheet.

TAKING YOUR LUNCH

It's not advisable to work during a lunch break. If hunger pains don't alert you to eat, at least have a healthy snack and a beverage. Brain food is just as important to have for adults as it is for students. If leaving the school and going out to sit in your car is permissible, a change in venue could do you some good. Whatever it takes to unwind for thirty minutes could make the difference between leaving the worksite with a great deal of stress or being energized knowing you earned your pay for the day because of your hard day's work.

If you choose to eat the school lunch, this should be fine for you. The food lately in the schools where I've worked hasn't been all that bad. It's fresh and hot. You won't have to worry about competing to use the microwave to warm up any foods you brought with you from home that requires microwaving. It's also a good idea to bring cash with you. Most cafeterias aren't equipped to take credit or debit cards. Very few will take a check. Too, if you want to sit with other teachers in the lounge, this would be a good idea to get your foot in the door and let them know how you feel about their school and the class you're working with. A good rule of thumb is never to say anything negative about the teacher or his students. By not doing this, you let them know you wouldn't do it to them if you subbed for them and ended up back in that same lounge talking to their colleagues.

At the end of your lunch, give yourself time to return the tray to the cafeteria, make any personal phone calls, and use the restroom. One of the hardest things about getting through the day for me was holding my urine. When no restroom is in the classroom for the students, they may be permitted to go use the restroom in cases of emergencies. The teacher or Substitute, though, must bear the burden of holding it and waiting until the students aren't in his care. During the lunch break, this is an especially appropriate time to do so.

LAST THREE HOURS

After the students are back in your care, they may have a little more energy than they had at the start of the day. It could be that many of them failed to eat breakfast or are just sluggish from not getting a full night's sleep from the night before. At any rate, it may be more of a challenge to deal with new behaviors and attitudes. Putting your foot down and reminding them of the rules you intend to enforce by any means necessary should keep them on track until that final bell rings and they're dismissed to their various transportation sites.

CLOSING THE DAY

The last full hour of the day should be a wrap-up of the day's activities, any take-home folders should be passed out, and a review of how each and every student gets home needs to be done. A wise course to follow is to go down your list of students still present and inquire about how he gets home. Changes could be made suddenly. Sometimes, they don't even know how they get home. If there are any uncertainties, calling or sending a quick note to the office with your inquiries may be a great research tool at this time. If their parents need to be called, you may be the one to do this. However, it's also noteworthy to understand that some children are products of broken homes. One parent may have custody and the other may not even be able to pick up the child. The child may not understand this and wouldn't mind going with a parent who may not be legally able to pick up the child. This poses a lot of responsibility on the Substitute. Also, you wouldn't want the child to miss the bus if he rode one. So, knowing well in advance how each child gets home will ensure the dismissal of each student goes smoothly and you're not held liable for one getting left behind or going to some place where he shouldn't be going.

Tidy up the room-especially the areas where you worked mainly such as the teacher's desk or table. If the room was already untidy when you arrived, a note to the teacher may want to be made on your Substitute Teacher's report. It could have been that the teacher had been out sick or on an extensive vacation for some emergent situation. Any other Substitutes could have caused the mess. Time may not have been available for you to do any additional cleaning during the course of your assignment, and it shouldn't fall on our shoulders to clean your mess and someone else's.

Erase and clean the chalkboard or whiteboard, and make sure your report is kept in a secure place where the teacher can find it and the students can't. Another Substitute Teacher, neighboring teacher, or even the principal may have to view it, so it should be easy to locate. The students shouldn't be able to get their hands on it, though. What's called "continuity of learning" is involved in your leaving an accurate report. The returning teacher would need to know what was taught and covered. Doing this will ensure the students have a smooth learning experience the following day as possible-just in case you don't go back to work with that same bunch of students.

Tip #3: Always make sure any students riding the bus are taken care of first as they could get left behind. You may have to stay late with them if this happens.

Tip #4: Always make sure the teacher's desk stays clean the whole day. Doing so ensures you won't have to rush at the end of the day to do any last-minute tidying.

SUMMARY

I hope these suggestions are workable for you and that you enjoy working in the field of Substitute Teaching as I have over the last ten years. Though dealing with classroom management can be challenging, it can be mastered with an understanding of the reasons why students have behaviors in order for you to be able to reach their hearts and win their respect. Have a sense of stick-to-it-iveness and let nothing get in your way of reaching your goals. -LaToya Jawara